£4.95

Overcoming Difficulties

GW00673696

Overcoming Difficulties

Wisdom from the Bahá'í Writings

by

Ginny Tod

George Ronald
Oxford

GEORGE RONALD, Publisher
46 High Street, Kidlington, Oxford OX5 2DN

*A catalogue record for this book is available
from the British Library*

ISBN 0–85398–481–6

Cover design by
Alexander Leith, *www.nineteenmedia.com*

Printed in Great Britain by
Cromwell Press Ltd, Trowbridge, Wilts BA14 0XB

Contents

Foreword

It has been said that we are like a baby in the 'world' of the womb. Just as the baby develops its physical arms and legs in the womb world so that it will be equipped for this one, so too are we developing our spiritual arms and legs in this world so that we will be equipped for the next one.

This physical world is not, in other words, an end in itself. It is the workroom for the next world, a place where we develop our spiritual capacities.

So what are our spiritual capacities and what do we need to develop them?

According to the world's holy books, our spiritual capacities are our virtues, i.e. kindness, consideration, understanding, forgiveness, respect, love, etc. These are qualities of the heart, gifted to us by God, that lie potentially within our soul, awaiting the right conditions for growth.

And the right conditions?

One of the conditions needed for their development are difficulties. Without difficulties our spiritual potential cannot be realized. For instance, our ability to love increases not when we are in a loving relationship but when we struggle to love someone we find difficult to love. Our virtue of patience develops not when everything is running smoothly but when we feel impatient and desire to get beyond these feelings. We forgive only after we have suffered the pain of hurt.

Bahá'u'lláh, the Founder of the Bahá'í Faith, said, '. . . God hath made adversity as a morning dew upon His green pasture . . .'[1]

Difficulties help our spiritual growth as the morning dew helps the growth of a plant and adds to the beauty of nature.

The other ingredient necessary for growth is will, our will. It is our decision whether or not we engage in the struggle of replacing feelings of aversion with feelings of love. We decide if we are going to work towards becoming more patient. The decision to forgive is ours.

The other component of growth is guidance, divine guidance. Without this we would not know how or why we need to reveal the gifts entrusted to our soul.

In summary, then, it can be said that our spiritual potential is realized via the dynamic interaction that takes place when we willingly engage in the struggle to fulfil God's guidance.

This book calls on a small portion of this guidance to help us in our work. In addition, the author at times uses her experience as a child psychotherapist and as a person who, like most, has faced difficulties to illustrate and highlight points raised in this guidance.

Overcoming Difficulties is for anyone engaged in the challenging yet enormously satisfying 'real' work of this world: to grow spiritually. This process not only enables us to contribute to the well-being of the planet but enables us at the point of our physical death to move, fully-equipped and well-prepared, to the next world.

Acknowledgements

I thank my husband Peter Jackson for all his help with this book; our son Nic Tod-Jackson for his sacrifices while I wrote it; my parents for their love, my dear sister for hers. I thank my friends for their unfailing support and the National Spiritual Assembly of the Bahá'ís of New Zealand for theirs.

1

Overcoming Grief and Suffering

Introduction

Often, major difficulties in life bring with them intense feelings of grief and sadness. So overwhelming can these feelings be that we may at times feel unable to carry on with our normal daily activities because of them. This in turn may trigger feelings of hopelessness and worthlessness.

It is for this reason that it is so important to have an understanding of the purpose of suffering, that is, a knowledge of why we suffer. This knowledge helps us 'see' our suffering in the context of the whole of our lives, including our life beyond this one. Thus our suffering can then be put into perspective. This in turn helps us to keep going with our lives, despite our suffering.

The quotations that follow are from 'Abdu'l-Bahá, the son of the Founder of the Bahá'í Faith, Bahá'u'lláh. Here 'Abdu'l-Bahá provides us with insights into the purpose of suffering, insights born from a man whose mind and heart were not only ever receptive to His father's divine teachings but who suffered 40 years of imprisonment and exile for following them.

When the winds blow severely,
rains fall fiercely, the lightning flashes, the thunder
roars, the bolt descends
and storms of trial become severe,
grieve not;
for after this storm, verily, the divine spring will
arrive,
the hills and fields will become verdant,
the expanses of grain will joyfully wave,
the earth will become covered with blossoms,
the trees will be clothed with green garments and
adorned with blossoms and fruits . . .
These favours are results of those storms and
hurricanes.
'Abdu'l-Bahá[1]

Men who suffer not, attain no perfection.
The plant most pruned by the gardeners
is that one which, when the summer comes,
will have the most beautiful blossoms
and the most abundant fruit.
'Abdu'l-Bahá[2]

The mind and spirit of man advance when he is tried
by suffering.
The more the ground is ploughed the better the seed
will grow, the better the harvest will be.
Just as the plough furrows the earth deeply,
purifying it of weeds and thistles,
so suffering and tribulation free man from the petty
affairs of this worldly life
until he arrives at a state of
complete detachment.
His attitude in this world will be that of divine
happiness.
Man is, so to speak, unripe:
the heat of the fire of suffering will mature him . . .
the greatest men have suffered most.
'Abdu'l-Bahá[3]

Those who suffer most, attain to the greatest
perfection.
'Abdu'l-Bahá[4]

It is likely that the people we admire most, have suffered
more than most.

The wisdom of the appearance of the spirit in the
body
is this:
the human spirit is a Divine Trust,
and it must traverse all conditions,
for its passage and movement
through the conditions of existence
will be the means of its acquiring perfections.
'Abdu'l-Bahá[5]

By moving through the condition of grief, it is likely that
we will become more compassionate, sensitive and caring
towards others. It is likely because grief renders us helpless
and vulnerable. This in turn helps us, when we become
stronger, to identify with other people's vulnerabilities.

৶ ৶ ৶

Do not grieve at the afflictions and calamities that
have befallen thee.
All calamities and afflictions have been created for
man
so that he may spurn this mortal world –
a world to which he is much attached.
When he experienceth severe trials and hardships,
then his nature will recoil and he will desire the
eternal realm –
a realm which is sanctified
from all afflictions and calamities.
'Abdu'l-Bahá[6]

We are at times, I think, like a young bird that is ready to fly (that is, ready to give up our earthly attachments) but which resists the prompting of its parent to leave the nest. However, just as the more powerful force of the parent bird overwhelms the younger one, pushing it from the nest, so too do severe trials and hardships overwhelm us. Then, while plummeting away from our earthly attachments towards what feels like certain destruction, we cry out to God, and just as the young bird discovers something that elevates it to heights previously unknown when living in the nest, so too do we. So pleasing are these heights that the things we once struggled to hang onto (for example, unhealthy relationships and behaviours, power, position or prestige) lose their appeal and a desire to 'keep flying' takes over.

I believe that when humanity begins to accept more fully the connection between mind and spirit, the understanding of the process of spiritual development occurring as a result of severe tests will be the fundmental basis for all psychological intervention; that is, psychological afflictions brought on by the stress of severe difficulties will be seen in the context of spiritual growth. Thus when a person presents himself to a practitioner with stress-related symptoms, prayer, meditation and support and guidance from friends will be part of his treatment plan.

Through suffering he will attain to an
eternal happiness which nothing can take from him.
'Abdu'l-Bahá[7]

Unfortunately, suffering has a bad name, particularly in the Western world. A friend of mine said recently, after the death of someone very close to her, that it felt as though society allowed her one day of sadness when he was buried and that was it.

What are we afraid of? Many indigenous cultures still practise ceremonies that reflect an understanding of the worth and process of suffering.

Has denial flourished in the white Western world because of our quest for comfort? Suffering is very uncomfortable but its benefits are profound.

To illustrate this, I call on the memory of a lovely woman who came to see me when I was practising child psychotherapy. She came because she was having problems with her young daughter. In an attempt to understand these problems I asked her for a family history. She began telling me about her other children and briefly mentioned a son who had died about three years prior to the birth of her daughter. I asked her about him and she began talking, for the first time in eight years, about his life and death. Apparently she had not wanted to burden anyone with her sadness at the time of his death.

Over a four to five week period this lady came to my office and wept so deeply that I am still greatly moved when I think about it. She brought photos of her son. She shared every small detail of his last night on earth and she cried, she cried very deeply, with a great deal of pain. However, in finally feeling her pain, in experiencing the rigours of the emotional storm grief brings with it, she was able to experience that calm that follows a storm. In that calm she experienced the eternal nature of life. Thus she experienced her son, who has never left life; thus she experienced peace. Interestingly, her problems with her daughter resolved almost as soon as this happened. Why? Because in her happiness and relief, she was able to feel love towards her daughter and it was this love that helped her daughter overcome her own difficulties.

2

Overcoming Anger and Hostility

Introduction

When the baby in the womb develops arms and legs, she is becoming equipped for life in this world. When we develop our spiritual arms and legs (i.e. our virtues) in this world we are preparing ourselves for life in the next.

We, however, have a choice about whether or not to develop our spiritual limbs, whereas the baby does not have a choice about developing her physical ones.

We choose whether or not we are going to be kind, patient and understanding or impatient, angry and hostile. We choose because God has provided us with free will. However, we also have understandings, given to us from God by way of His divine Messengers, that He desires and expects us to overcome these less noble emotions.

So how do we, if we choose to, overcome the conditions of hate, envy, anger, hostility and so on? Fortunately, God in His mercy has provided us with detailed information on this, information that has throughout the ages been supplied to humanity at intervals of approximately five hundred to a thousand years through His divine Messengers.

Following are quotations taken from the writings of Bahá'u'lláh, God's latest Messenger, and 'Abdu'l-Bahá, the greatest Exemplar of His teachings. These quotations not only provide us with a standard towards which God desires us to rise but guidance as to how to do so, a process, we will see, that strengthens our 'spiritual arms and legs'.

. . . love is light, no matter in what abode it dwelleth;
and hate is darkness, no matter where it may make its
nest.

'Abdu'l-Bahá[1]

If we have suffered because of another person's actions,
we may feel bitter and angry towards him. This is natural
but if we do not move beyond these feelings, they may
damage us more than the actions of the person who trig-
gered them. In other words, if we harbour feelings of
hate and bitterness we may endanger our soul and
consign it to darkness.

I have found that doing battle with my anger, in an
attempt to overcome it, rarely works. This is because, I
believe, that just as an angry child desires to be heard, so
too do our adult angry feelings. If we try to suppress our
anger it seems to come back with a vengeance. If,
however, we take ourselves away from the situation that
set off our anger – preferably before entering into a
verbal attack – give ourselves permission to reveal our
anger to ourselves *without judgement*, then it is likely that
our anger will diminish. For just as an angry child begins
to calm down if her angry feelings are listened to, so too
do ours.

In other words, respecting our feelings – calling on our
virtue of respect for self – helps in the process of
reducing anger. Once reduced, we are in a position to
deal with the person who sparked off our anger in a way
that will not set off theirs.

❧   ❧   ❧

Verily the most necessary thing is contentment under
all circumstances;
by this one is preserved from morbid conditions and
from lassitude.
Yield not to grief and sorrow:
they cause the greatest misery.
Jealously consumeth the body
and anger doth burn the liver:
avoid these two as you would a lion.

Bahá'u'lláh[2]

Without contentment in our lives, without a sense of
purpose and direction which facilitates contentment, we
are prone to feelings of insecurity or jealously, frustration
or anger.

Discovering what we enjoy doing in life; finding a
profession that incorporates our likes; setting ourselves
goals in relation to our work; working steadily towards
our goals; feeding our soul with spiritual food: these
things counteract feelings of insecurity, jealously, frustration and anger.

❧   ❧   ❧

The individual must be educated to such a high
degree
that he . . . would think it easier to be slashed with a
sword
or pierced with a spear
than to utter calumny or be carried away by wrath.

'Abdu'l-Bahá[3]

How many marriages would be saved, how many children spared the confusion and anxiety of listening to their parents argue, if this were so?

How many children would be protected from the torment of school bullying if this were so?

How many lives would be saved from the horrors of war if this were so?

If he exercises his anger and wrath
against the bloodthirsty tyrants
who are like ferocious beasts,
it is very praiseworthy;
but if he does not use these qualities in a right way,
they are blameworthy.
'Abdu'l-Bahá[4]

Blessed are such as hold fast to the cord of kindliness
and tender mercy and are free from
animosity and hatred.
Bahá'u'lláh[5]

A friend of mine, the grandchild of black slaves, was raised in a country that practised segregation. She lost her mother when she was nine. Not long after her husband died in her middle age, she suffered a brutal physical attack. Yet she held 'fast to the cord of kindliness and tender mercy'. My friend died in her eighties and at her funeral her son-in-law said that in the 20 years he had known her, he had never heard her speak unkindly about anyone. He called her a 'five foot spiritual giant; a spiritual eagle who walked with a walking stick'.

Our children, unless they are helped to think differently, will consider that success is being a pop, movie or sports star – usually with few clothes on. They will think this because this is what is portrayed as successful in today's world. Role models generally do not take the form of a little five foot woman with a walking stick – unless we point out to our children the greatness of women and men such as my friend.

❧ ❧ ❧

Be not the cause of grief, much less of discord and strife.
Bahá'u'lláh[6]

What a lot of work we must do, in our hearts and minds, before we can express our dissatisfaction about something, in a constructive, positive and loving way!

❧ ❧ ❧

Illumine and hallow your hearts;
let them not be profaned by the thorns of hate or the thistles of malice . . .
Blessed is he who mingleth with all men
in a spirit of utmost kindliness and love.
Bahá'u'lláh[7]

> Breathe not the sins of others
> so long as thou art thyself a sinner.
> Shouldst thou transgress this command,
> accursed wouldst thou be . . .
> *Bahá'u'lláh*[8]

One of the greatest battles that ever rages happens, I believe, within the heart of someone who has been upset by another but who is determined not to speak unkindly about that person. If she wins this battle, she has won a major spiritual victory.

> Act in such a way that your heart may be free from hatred.
> *'Abdu'l-Bahá*[9]

Knowledge of what one likes doing in life, what one would like to achieve, setting goals in relation to this, developing healthy spiritual practices, following divine guidance helps us to act in such a way that our heart is free from hatred.

> Pay ye no heed to aversion and rejection,
> to disdain, hostility, injustice:
> act ye in the opposite way.
> *'Abdu'l-Bahá*[10]

. . . we must see neither harshness nor injustice,
neither malevolence, nor hostility, nor hate,
but rather turn our eyes
toward the heaven of ancient glory.
'Abdu'l-Bahá[11]

∽ ∽ ∽

Should any come to blows with you, seek to be
friends with him;
should any stab you to the heart, be ye a healing salve
unto his sores;
should any taunt and mock at you, meet him with
love.
Should any heap his blame upon you, praise ye him;
should he offer you a deadly poison, give him the
choicest honey in exchange;
and should he threaten your life, grant him a remedy
that will heal him evermore.
Should he be pain itself, be ye his medicine;
should he be thorns, be ye his roses and sweet herbs.
'Abdu'l-Bahá[12]

∽ ∽ ∽

Think ye of love and good fellowship
as the delights of heaven,
think ye of hostility and hatred
as the torments of hell.
'Abdu'l-Bahá[13]

I have noticed that when I get angry or irritated with someone, I am the one who feels unhappy. I have also noticed that if I manage to forgive that person, my problems with her fade, as do my anger and irritation.

Heaven and hell, it would seem, are not places but states of the mind and heart.

A thought of hatred must be destroyed
by a more powerful
thought of love.
'Abdu'l-Bahá[14]

Sincerity and love will conquer hate.
'Abdu'l-Bahá[15]

3

Overcoming Fear

Introduction

The fear of a child, alone at night, afraid of the dark, will only diminish when loving arms comfort him. Likewise, only when adults experience comfort will their fears decrease.

Divine comfort, the most enduring and profound of all comforts, is experienced within the heart. Thus the more we turn our heart to the divine, the more comfort we will experience and the less fear we will suffer.

Whatever decreaseth fear increaseth courage.
Bahá'u'lláh[1]

The Báb, one of the leading figures of my Faith, was travelling on a small boat for many days in violent seas. So bad were the conditions that the crew feared for their lives. The Báb, however, having committed all to God, was at perfect peace.

When fear and anxiety overwhelm me, I imagine I am sitting with Him on that boat in stormy seas and I calm down.

Be not afraid of anyone, place thy whole trust in God, the Almighty, the All-Knowing.
Bahá'u'lláh[2]

How free I feel when I manage to do this.

Be not afraid of anyone, place thy whole trust in God,
the Almighty, the All-Knowing.

. . . they have said:
'Love is a light
that never dwelleth in a heart
possessed by fear.'
Bahá'u'lláh[3]

Once a four-year-old boy came to the clinic where I was working. His mother was finding him difficult to manage and was seeking help. We heard how this young boy had witnessed the death of his father in a tragic accident, how his mother had tried hard to keep the family business going after her husband's death while at the same time looking after her two shocked children. The family was very distressed.

It was decided that part of the treatment for this family would include a therapist seeing the young boy in a specially designed playroom. This room was furnished with toys and equipment that help children express their feelings. I was very fortunate to be the therapist who worked with this boy. While there I learned how vividly our thoughts affect our behaviour, how our fears decrease when we safely assimilate them and that, when we do, how much more available we are to loving others and being loved ourselves.

For whatever reason, this particular young boy felt perfectly at home in the playroom as soon as he entered: he immediately began playing in a way that clearly expressed his deepest thoughts about himself and his experiences. During the hours I was with him, I felt like I was an observer within his dream. He disclosed, during our time together, that he felt he had killed his father. This is not an uncommon belief in young children whose parents have died. Children naturally feel that the world revolves around them and that they are the instigators of both the good and the bad things that happen to them. This child also revealed his fear of the terrible things that were 'after' him because he was such a bad person. I did not need to reassure him directly or help him to change his beliefs about himself, for he did all this himself. All I had to do was ensure he had a safe, non-judgemental environment in which he could assimilate his feelings. The stressful environment in which he lived after his father's death, although perfectly understandable, contributed to his negative, harsh thoughts about himself. By finding a safe place in which he could process his thoughts and feelings, he came to understandings about himself that were much less bitter and punitive, which in turn lessened his 'manic' behaviour. Although he did all the work, he attributed his improved feelings to me, for he explained at the end of his last session that a doctor had given a shark a teaspoon of medicine and the shark wasn't dangerous anymore. After talking to his mother (who also received help) some months later I learned that the young boy and his family were doing well.

'Abdu'l-Bahá exhorts us to spend much time in prayer and meditation. I believe when we do this we create a safe environment for ourselves, within ourselves, that neutralizes our harsh, punitive thoughts about ourselves and others – thoughts that increase our anxieties and fears, thoughts that are the outcome of stressful events and circumstances. If we are consumed with fear and anxiety, we may need to increase the time we spend in prayer and meditation.

૭ ૭ ૭

Were men to discover
the motivating purpose
of God's Revelation,
they would assuredly cast away their fears,
and, with hearts filled with gratitude,
rejoice with exceeding gladness.
Bahá'u'lláh[4]

Let not fear fall upon you,
neither be troubled nor dismayed.
Take ye good heed
lest this calamitous day
slacken the flames of your ardour,
and quench your tender hopes.
Today is the day for steadfastness and constancy.
Blessed are they
that stand firm and immovable as the rock
and brave the storm and stress
of this tempestuous hour.

'Abdu'l-Bahá[5]

I once met a woman whose life was in disarray. Her husband of many years was planning to leave her for another women. She was very scared but she also possessed strong virtues of dignity and courage.

As difficult as it was to do, she called on these virtues, these gifts from God, to help her get beyond her problem. She set herself a goal. She decided she was not going to try to influence her husband's decision, nor was she going to expend any energy arguing. Instead, she decided to pursue a dream she had had for many years about her own career.

Then her husband changed his mind. They stayed together but she continued with her dreams. Even if he had left her, I suspect that her personal strengths would have saved her from despair.

෯ ෯ ෯

. . . be thou so steadfast in My love
that thy heart shall not waver,
even if the swords of the enemies rain blows upon
thee
and all the heavens and the earth arise against thee.

Bahá'u'lláh[6]

4

Developing Patience

Introduction

A newborn infant has no patience. When he is hungry he
will cry out in distress. If, however, he is always fed when
hungry and if he develops normally, he will over time be
able to wait for his food, for short periods of time, even if
hungry.

This happens because he becomes old enough and
experienced enough to trust that he will eventually be
fed. In other words, his experience of trust facilitates his
capacity to be patient.

It is the same for adults. Our ability to be patient
during difficulties is determined by our capacity to trust
that relief will eventually come. Thus patience and trust
can be seen as inextricably linked together.

As we grow in trust, so too does our capacity to be
patient increase. And it is important that it does, for
patience protects us from agitation, an emotion that
wreaks havoc on our minds, bodies and the people
around us.

Be patient, for thy Lord is patient.
Bahá'u'lláh[1]

When I feel impatient and angry with others, it helps me to reflect on the unwise things I have said and done in my life and to remember how patient my Father in heaven has been with me.

Blessed are the steadfastly enduring,
they that are patient under ills and hardships,
who lament not over anything that befalleth them,
and who tread the path of resignation . . .
Bahá'u'lláh[2]

Let thine heart be patient, and be thou not dismayed.
Follow not in the way of them that are sorely
agitated.
Bahá'u'lláh[3]

The virtues and attributes pertaining unto God are all
evident and manifest,
and have been mentioned and described in all the
heavenly Books.
Among them are

trustworthiness, truthfulness, purity of heart while
communing with God,
forbearance, resignation to whatever the Almighty
hath decreed,
contentment with the things His Will hath provided,
patience, nay, thankfulness in the midst of tribulation,
and complete reliance, in all circumstances, upon
Him.
These rank, according to the estimate of God,
among the highest and most laudable of all acts.

Bahá'u'lláh[4]

. . . patiently endure thy sorrows.

Bahá'u'lláh[5]

I have found that I can only patiently endure my sorrows
if I immerse myself in prayer and study of the holy
words. If I do not do this, then my sorrows quickly overwhelm me.

He will, certainly, repay all them
that endure with patience
and put their confidence in Him.

Bahá'u'lláh[6]

If anyone revile you, or trouble touch you,
in the path of God,
be patient,
and put your trust in Him
Who heareth, Who seeth.
Bahá'u'lláh[7]

. . . be patient in the hour of loss.
Adversity is followed by success
and rejoicings follow woe.
Bahá'u'lláh[8]

And if he meeteth with injustice
he shall have patience,
and if he cometh upon wrath
he shall manifest love.
Bahá'u'lláh[9]

What an enormously difficult task this is. But it is, I have
discovered – the hard way – the only way to really resolve
conflict.

I have found that if I verbally attack someone who
has upset me, I end up feeling depleted, hateful and
angry, and nothing gets resolved. If, however, I somehow
hang onto the virtue of patience, move away from the
situation, seek to find love in my heart for the person
who antagonized me, then I calm down and I am able

to sort things out with that person peacefully.
Patience should not be mistaken for passivity.

. . . this earthly life shall come to an end,
and everyone shall expire and return unto my Lord
God
Who will reward with the choicest gifts
the deeds of those who endure with patience.
The Báb[10]

When calamity striketh, be ye patient and composed.
'Abdu'l-Bahá[11]

. . . manifest magnificent patience during every
calamity and hardship.
'Abdu'l-Bahá[12]

5

Developing Hope and Assurance

Introduction

By their very nature difficulties are hard to bear. If they were not, we would not be motivated to cry out to God for help while facing them and we would not experience feelings of thankfulness, love and fulfilment that His response to our cry generates within us.

Nor would we develop our virtue of trust. For trust arises from the recognition that relief from distress will eventually come, a recognition gained by way of successive experiences of having being relieved.

Difficulties not only provide us with the opportunity to experience God's loving mercy in all its forms but they enable us to develop our virtues. However, as we know difficulties are hard to bear, so divine words that help and comfort us while we are facing them are essential to the happiness of our soul.

Set all thy hope in God,
and cleave tenaciously
to His unfailing mercy.
Bahá'u'lláh[1]

The wonders of His bounty can never cease,
and the stream of His merciful grace
can never be arrested.
Bahá'u'lláh[2]

. . . be thou not hopeless under any circumstances,
but rather be firm in thy hope.
'Abdu'l-Bahá[3]

If we begin to feel feelings of despondency rising up within us, then it may be important to increase the time we spend in prayer and meditation.

This became apparent to me when I increased my prayer time after feeling despondent for a long period.

Nothing save that which profiteth them
can befall My loved ones.
Bahá'u'lláh[4]

Every day advertising bombards us with the idea that our lives will improve if we look a certain way or buy a certain product. God outdoes this. He says that anything we experience in life, be it good or bad, will profit us – providing, that is, we are one of His loved ones.

What efforts do I need to make to become a loved one of God?

❧ ❧ ❧

Heed not your weaknesses and frailty;
fix your gaze
upon the invincible power of the Lord,
your God, the Almighty . . .
Arise in His name,
put your trust wholly in Him,
and be assured of ultimate victory.
The Báb[5]

When I am struggling with my own sense of impotence and powerlessness, I remember this and I am filled with an energy which I know is not from me.

❧ ❧ ❧

He will never deal unjustly with anyone,
neither will He task a soul beyond its power.
Bahá'u'lláh[6]

Remember not your own limitations;
the help of God will come to you.
Forget yourself.
God's help will surely come!
'Abdu'l-Bahá[7]

❧   ❧   ❧

No capacity is limited when led by the Spirit of God!
'Abdu'l-Bahá[8]

One night I had a very clear dream that helped me understand the significance of this passage.

In this dream I saw an old-fashioned cigar-shaped rocket that I knew represented me. It was spluttering along, obviously just about out of fuel. It was in poor shape and it was clear that it was not very effective or efficient.

In front of it appeared a most glorious looking space ship. It was white and beautiful and had a large opening that I knew I could pass through if I wished. I did so, fearful that I would blow up the beautiful craft. However, this did not happen.

As soon as I was inside, the craft flew off, flying with indescribable power and beauty. It was clear that there was no comparison between the pathetic rocket that was me and this craft. They were two distinct entities. One had power and beauty, the other did not.

This dream helped me to understand my powerlessness in relation to God, my inability to do very much or be very effective without Him. It also enabled me to appreciate that He allows me to be helped by His power.

The omnipotence of God
shall solve every difficulty.
'Abdu'l-Bahá[9]

I believe this is why the holy writings exhort us to be patient under every ordeal. If we are patient, we experience the omnipotent 'hand' of God solving our difficulties. If we jump up and down, complain and moan, we do not provide the space in our hearts for the omnipotent power to influence our lives.

6

Using Prayer

Introduction

Spiritual malnutrition generates feelings of loneliness, isolation, frustration and despair. Spiritual food disperses these feelings.

> At the dawn of every day
> he should commune with God, and,
> with all his soul,
> persevere in the quest of his Beloved.
> *Bahá'u'lláh*[1]

What a difference putting aside more time to say my prayers has made to my life. I am not as grumpy in the mornings, I laugh more, I feel more assured.

ॐ ॐ ॐ

> Whoso reciteth, in the privacy of his chamber,
> the verses revealed by God,
> the scattering angels of the Almighty
> shall scatter abroad the fragrance of the words
> uttered by his mouth . . .
> *Bahá'u'lláh*[2]

ॐ ॐ ॐ

> The most acceptable prayer
> is the one offered with the utmost spirituality and
> radiance;
> its prolongation hath not been and is not beloved by
> God.
> The more detached and the purer the prayer,
> the more acceptable is it in the presence of God.
> *The Báb*[3]

Once, when I was alone after listening to an adult friend

describe the shocking injustice she had experienced as a child at the hands of her father, I cried out, 'Help me God.' I was overcome with the injustice she had suffered and that so many children continue to suffer.

That night, after going to bed, still feeling tormented, I had a dream. My friend was in a garden but it wasn't made up of ordinary plants. The flowers and the tree in this garden had a vibrant energy to them, an energy that can best be described as light and love. When I looked at my friend in that garden she radiated love and somehow I knew her garden had been created as a result of her love.

I had been shown, I believe as a result of my short, desperate prayer, that my friend had or would transcend the horrors of her childhood at some point in her existence.

And although I do not believe we should stop for one moment doing whatever we can in this world to alleviate the suffering of children, my dream did provide me with assurance that healing will occur, be it in this world or the next, for the hundreds and thousands of children presently suffering at the hands of adults who are out of control.

❦   ❦   ❦

. . . whatever we ask for which is in accord with
divine wisdom,
God will answer.
. . . In His mercy He answers the prayers of all His
servants
when according to His supreme wisdom it is necessary.
'Abdu'l-Bahá[4]

God Who has given the revelation to His Prophets
will surely give of His abundance
daily bread to all those who ask Him faithfully.
'Abdu'l-Bahá[5]

Pray to God
that He may strengthen you in divine virtue,
so that you may be as angels in the world . . .
'Abdu'l-Bahá[6]

If we are sick and in distress
let us implore God's healing,
and He will answer our prayer.
'Abdu'l-Bahá[7]

. . . with every soul who is attracted to the Kingdom
of God,
his greatest hope
is to find an opportunity to entreat and supplicate
before his Beloved,
appeal for His mercy and grace and be immersed in
the ocean of His utterance,
goodness and generosity.
'Abdu'l-Bahá[8]

The state of prayer is the best of conditions,
for man is then associating with God.
Prayer verily bestoweth life,
particularly when offered in private
and at times, such as midnight, when freed from daily
cares.
'Abdu'l-Bahá[9]

Take courage!
God never forsakes His children
who strive and work and pray!
'Abdu'l-Bahá[10]

The wisdom of prayer is this:
That it causeth a connection
between the servant and the True One,
because in that state man with all heart and soul
turneth his face towards His Highness the Almighty,
seeking His association and desiring His love and
compassion.
'Abdu'l-Bahá[11]

When we ring up a friend and ask for her advice, we do
not put the phone down before hearing it. Nor should we
get up too quickly after praying. It pays to sit in quiet
contemplation after we have prayed to hear what comes
into our heart.

Rely upon God.
Trust in Him. Praise Him,
and call Him continually to mind.
He verily turneth trouble into ease,
and sorrow into solace, and toil into utter peace.
He verily hath dominion over all things.
'Abdu'l-Bahá[12]

Once when I was practising psychotherapy, a distressed man phoned me to say that his five-year-old said she wanted to die (her mother had just left the family to live with another man). I guessed the little girl wanted to die because her feelings of shock, grief and anxiety were consuming her – dying is often seen as a way of avoiding these feelings, even in the very young. With this in mind I told the man to tell his daughter I would see her so long as she brought all her horrible feelings with her. I said this so that she would have hope that something could be done with them. When we are flooded with grief and anxiety, we usually feel nothing can be done to help us, which in turn adds to our problem.

The little girl arrived at the clinic looking pale and anxious. She left her father hesitantly and came inside with me. Once inside, I asked her to draw everything she was feeling. She picked up a black crayon and began to draw. Her drawings were dark and very grim. Then, after a considerable time, she stopped, put down her crayon, stood up, looked around the room as if seeing it for the first time and in a cheerful voice said that she hoped her father would remember to buy her an ice cream! The little girl had faced her terror and was free.

The little girl was helped, I believe, because she trusted someone with her fear and in doing so she was relieved of it. If we share our fear, pain, hurt or frustration with God, in the same spirit of trust that the little girl shared with me, then I believe we will experience a similar sort of relief.

On some occasions when I have felt overwhelmed by my distress, I have said to myself, 'Right, you are going into your room, you are going to say prayers and you are not coming out until you feel better.' It has always worked. I have always come away from those prayer sessions relieved of my distress. I believe it works because by saying 'you are not coming out until you feel better' I provide myself with hope that something can be done to help me feel better. This in turn reduces my anxiety and I become available to the healing within the prayers, healing that is always there but which my anxiety has prevented me from accessing.

On other occasions when my pain or frustration over-powers me, I have found that it helps if I allow it to overwhelm me – so long as I believe that as I am being swamped by it, the All-Knowing, All-Loving Creator is with me.

Alternatively, I have found it helpful to find a symbol in my mind that represents my anguish: a broken or damaged object, a bleeding wound or the like. I then show this symbol in my mind to God, trusting that He is looking at it at the same time I am.

ৰ্ঙ   ৰ্ঙ   ৰ্ঙ

Blessed the distressed one
who seeketh refuge beneath the shadow of My
canopy.
Bahá'u'lláh[13]

Is there any Remover of difficulties save God?
Say: Praised be God!
He is God!
All are His servants, and all abide by His bidding!
The Báb[14]

❧   ❧   ❧

Thy name is my healing, O my God,
and remembrance of Thee is my remedy.
Nearness to Thee is my hope,
and love for Thee is my companion.
Thy mercy to me is my healing and my succour
in both this world and the world to come.
Thou, verily, art the All-Bountiful, the All-Knowing,
the All-Wise.
Bahá'u'lláh[15]

❧   ❧   ❧

Suffer me, O my God, to draw nigh unto Thee,
and to abide within the precincts of Thy court,
for remoteness from Thee hath well-nigh consumed
me.
Cause me to rest under the shadow of the wings of
Thy grace,
for the flame of my separation from Thee
hath melted my heart within me.
Draw me nearer unto the river that is life indeed,
for my soul burneth with thirst
in its ceaseless search after Thee.

My sighs, O my God, proclaim the bitterness of mine
anguish,
and the tears I shed attest my love for Thee.
I beseech Thee,
by the praise wherewith Thou praisest Thyself
and the glory wherewith Thou glorifiest Thine own
Essence,
to grant that we may be numbered among them
that have recognized Thee
and acknowledged Thy sovereignty in Thy days.
Help us then to quaff, O my God,
from the fingers of mercy
the living waters of Thy loving-kindness,
that we may utterly forget all else except Thee,
and be occupied only with Thy Self.
Powerful art Thou to do what Thou willest.
No God is there beside Thee,
the Mighty, the Help in Peril, the Self-Subsisting.
Glorified be Thy name, O Thou Who art the King of
all Kings!

Bahá'u'lláh[16]

7
Healing

Introduction

A major difficulty we face in life is physical, emotional or mental illness, if not personally then in someone close to us. As well as this intimate experience of illness, we are presently living in a world generally bereft of health.

Children in one country die of malnutrition, brought on by decades of civil war. Young people with enough food in another kill themselves because they lack hope and faith. Pollution is pumped into an already ailing environment, with rivers, lakes, seas, animals and humans dying because of it. People trapped in their passions and prejudices maim and harm others. Rainforests, the source of our oxygen, are being burnt down at alarming rates. We are not a well world.

Transcending unwellness is difficult, be it on an individual or a global level. But it is not impossible, with the right medicines. With divine guidance and unity of thought and mind, the world's troubles will eventually be overcome. With trust, faith, hope and medical intervention, where necessary, an individual's health can improve. And like all difficulties, illness provides us with an opportunity to grow and develop spiritually, be it individually or collectively.

There are two ways of healing sickness,
material means and spiritual means.
The first is by the use of remedies, of medicines;
the second consists in praying to God and in turning
to Him.
Both means should be used and practised.
Illness caused by physical accident should be treated
with medical remedies;
those which are due to spiritual causes disappear
through spiritual means.
Thus an illness caused by affliction, fear, nervous
impressions,
will be healed by spiritual rather than by physical
treatment.
Hence, both kinds of remedies should be considered.

'Abdu'l-Bahá[1]

If thou art desirous of health,
wish thou health for serving the Kingdom.

'Abdu'l-Bahá[2]

It is interesting how our aliments can be ameliorated
when our attention is focused on something bigger than
ourselves.

Now, if thou wishest to know the true remedy
which will heal man from all sickness

and will give him the health of the divine kingdom,
know that it is the precepts and teachings of God.
Focus thine attention upon them.
'Abdu'l-Bahá[3]

I began to see while practising psychotherapy that the ills
affecting society were caused by a lack of commitment to
spiritual principles and laws.

For instance, the sexually abused youngster was abused
because his or her father or mother, uncle or aunt, grand-
father or other person had no or little appreciation that
he or she was created by God, was here to develop spiritual 'arms and legs' and would return to Him at death.
Without this appreciation this person became a victim of
his own desires. Propelled by his physical urges, he
carried out acts that had tragic consequences for others.

Psychological intervention to help heal the trauma of
abuse is imperative. But until society begins to live by the
'precepts and teachings of God', abuse will not stop.

. . . the Teachings of God are as healing balm,
a medicine for the conscience of man.
They clear the head,
so that a man can breathe them in
and delight in their sweet fragrance.
'Abdu'l-Bahá[4]

. . . if the spiritual health is afflicted with the love of
the world,
spiritual medicine must be given.
These medicines are the advices and commands of
God,
which will have effect upon it.
'Abdu'l-Bahá[5]

❧   ❧   ❧

All true healing comes from God!
There are two causes for sickness,
one is material, the other spiritual.
If the sickness is of the body, a material remedy is
needed,
if of the soul, a spiritual remedy.
'Abdu'l-Bahá[6]

For Bahá'ís, spiritual remedies come in the form of
prayer, meditation on the word of God, obedience to that
word and service to others.

❧   ❧   ❧

The Prophets of God should be regarded as
physicians
whose task is to foster the well-being of the world and
its peoples,
that, through the spirit of oneness,
they may heal the sickness of a divided humanity.
Bahá'u'lláh[7]

The whole of mankind is in the grip of manifold ills.
Strive, therefore, to save its life
through the wholesome medicine
which the almighty hand of the unerring Physician
hath prepared.

Bahá'u'lláh[8]

   ᔰ   ᔰ   ᔰ

The Prophets and Messengers of God
have been sent down for the sole purpose
of guiding mankind to the straight Path of Truth.
The purpose underlying Their revelation hath been
to educate all men,
that they may, at the hour of death,
ascend, in the utmost purity and sanctity and with
absolute detachment,
to the throne of the Most High.

Bahá'u'lláh[9]

8

The Next World

Introduction

Just as a child goes from one class to the next, building on the knowledge of the previous class, so too does humanity. Humanity advances in knowledge and understanding in exactly the same way that a child does at school. However, instead of human teachers being responsible for this learning, divine ones are.

Divine teachers appointed by God help humanity advance to the next stage of its development – divine teachers known to us by the names Krishna, Moses, Zoroaster, Buddha, Jesus Christ, Muḥammad, the Báb and Bahá'u'lláh. Each teacher supplies humanity with information that helps it develop both materially and spiritually. Each one appears on earth at a point when humanity has progressed to a level where new guidance is required.

Each teacher also tells us something of the next world. Here are the words of Bahá'u'lláh and His son 'Abdu'l-Bahá on this subject.

Know thou of a truth that the soul, after its separation from the body, will continue to progress until it attaineth the presence of God, in a state and condition which neither the revolution of ages and centuries, nor the changes and chances of this world, can alter. It will endure as long as the Kingdom of God, His sovereignty, His dominion and power will endure. It will manifest the signs of God and His attributes, and will reveal His loving-kindness and bounty. The movement of My Pen is stilled when it attempteth to befittingly describe the loftiness and glory of so exalted a station. The honour with which the Hand of Mercy will invest the soul is such as no tongue can adequately reveal, nor any other earthly agency describe. Blessed is the soul which, at the hour of its separation from the body, is sanctified from the vain imaginings of the peoples of the world. Such a soul liveth and moveth in accordance with the Will of its Creator, and entereth the all-highest Paradise. The Maids of Heaven, inmates of the loftiest mansions, will circle around it, and the Prophets of God and His chosen ones will seek its companionship. With them that soul will freely converse, and will recount unto them that which it hath been made to endure in the path of God, the Lord of all worlds. If any man be told that which hath been ordained for such a soul in the worlds of God, the Lord of the throne on high and of earth below, his whole being will instantly blaze out in his great longing to attain that most exalted, that sanctified and resplendent station . . . The nature of the soul after death can never be described, nor is it meet and permissible to reveal its whole character to the eyes of men. The Prophets and Messengers of God have been

sent down for the sole purpose of guiding mankind to
the straight Path of Truth. The purpose underlying
Their revelation hath been to educate all men, that
they may, at the hour of death, ascend, in the utmost
purity and sanctity and with absolute detachment, to
the throne of the Most High. The light which these
souls radiate is responsible for the progress of the
world and the advancement of its peoples. They are
like unto leaven which leaveneth the world of being,
and constitute the animating force through which the
arts and wonders of the world are made manifest.
Through them the clouds rain their bounty upon men,
and the earth bringeth forth its fruits. All things must
needs have a cause, a motive power, an animating
principle. These souls and symbols of detachment
have provided, and will continue to provide, the
supreme moving impulse in the world of being. The
world beyond is as different from this world as this
world is different from that of the child while still in the
womb of its mother. When the soul attaineth the
Presence of God, it will assume the form that best
befitteth its immortality and is worthy of its celestial
habitation.

Bahá'u'lláh[1]

As to thy question regarding discoveries made by the
soul after it hath put off its human form: certainly, that
world is a world of perceptions and discoveries, for the
interposed veil will be lifted away and the human spirit
will gaze upon souls that are above, below, and on a

par with itself. It is similar to the condition of a human being in the womb, where his eyes are veiled, and all things are hidden away from him. Once he is born out of the uterine world and entereth this life, he findeth it, with relation to that of the womb, to be a place of perceptions and discoveries, and he observeth all things through his outer eye. In the same way, once he hath departed this life, he will behold, in that world whatsoever was hidden from him here: but there he will look upon and comprehend all things with his inner eye.

'Abdu'l-Bahá[2]

O thou beloved maid-servant of God, although the loss of a son is indeed heart-breaking and beyond the limits of human endurance, yet one who knoweth and understandeth is assured that the son hath not been lost but, rather, hath stepped from this world into another, and she will find him in the divine realm. That reunion shall be for eternity, while in this world separation is inevitable and bringeth with it a burning grief.

Praise be unto God that thou hast faith, art turning thy face toward the everlasting Kingdom and believest in the existence of a heavenly world. Therefore be thou not disconsolate, do not languish, do not sigh, neither wail nor weep; for agitation and mourning deeply affect his soul in the divine realm.

That beloved child addresseth thee from the hidden world: 'O thou kind Mother, thank divine Providence that I have been freed from a small and gloomy cage and, like the birds of the meadows, have soared to the divine world – a world which is spacious, illumined, and ever gay and jubilant. Therefore, lament not, O Mother, and be not grieved; I am not of the lost, nor have I been obliterated and destroyed. I have shaken off the mortal form and have raised my banner in this spiritual world. Following this separation is everlasting companionship. Thou shalt find me in the heaven of the Lord, immersed in an ocean of light.'

'Abdu'l-Bahá[3]

A friend shared with me how she had felt extremely sad about the loss of her mother until she started to visualize meeting up with her again in the next world.

9

Conclusion

Conclusion

Our life in this world is short. Compared to eternity we are here for less time than it takes to blink an eye. But there is important work to do. We must, if we want to be happy in this world, contribute to its well-being, develop our spiritual arms and legs for the next world and replace anger with love, hopelessness with confidence and disquiet with patience.

But how do we do this? How do we change our sometimes forceful, violent, overwhelming feelings into smooth, enriching, life-giving ones? We do it by following the guidance given to us by God through His divine Messenger.

The quotations in this book represent a tiny drop out of an ocean of His words but a drop that may help us on our journey in all the worlds of God, including our journey through this one.

Bibliography

'Abdu'l-Bahá. *Paris Talks*. London: Bahá'í Publishing Trust, 1967.
—— *The Promulgation of Universal Peace*. Wilmette, IL: Bahá'í Publishing Trust, 1982.
—— *Selections from the Writings of 'Abdu'l-Bahá*. Haifa: Bahá'í World Centre, 1978.
—— *Some Answered Questions*. Wilmette, IL: Bahá'í Publishing Trust, 1981.
The Báb. *Selections from the Writings of the Báb*. Haifa: Bahá'í World Centre, 1976.
Bahá'í Prayers: A Selection of Prayers revealed by Bahá'u'lláh, the Báb and 'Abdu'l-Bahá. Wilmette, IL: Bahá'í Publishing Trust, 1991.
Bahá'í World Faith. Wilmette, IL: Bahá'í Publishing Trust, 2nd edn. 1976.
Bahá'u'lláh. *Epistle to the Son of the Wolf*. Wilmette, IL: Bahá'í Publishing Trust, 1988.
—— *Gleanings from the Writings of Bahá'u'lláh*. Wilmette, IL: Bahá'í Publishing Trust, 1983.
—— *The Hidden Words*. Wilmette, IL: Bahá'í Publishing Trust, 1990.
—— *Prayers and Meditations*. Wilmette, IL: Bahá'í Publishing Trust, 1987.
—— *The Seven Valleys and the Four Valleys*. Wilmette, IL: Bahá'í Publishing Trust, 1991.
—— *Tablets of Bahá'u'lláh revealed after the Kitáb-i-Aqdas*. Haifa: Bahá'í World Centre, 1978.
Compilation of Compilations, The. Prepared by the Universal House of Justice 1963–1990. 2 vols. [Sydney]: Bahá'í Publications Australia, 1991.

Nabíl-i-A'ẓam. *The Dawn-Breakers: Nabíl's Narrative of the Early Days of the Bahá'í Revelation*. Wilmette, IL: Bahá'í Publishing Trust, 1970.

Shoghi Effendi. *The Advent of Divine Justice*. Wilmette, IL: Bahá'í Publishing Trust, 1990.

Star of the West. rpt. Oxford: George Ronald, 1984.

References

Foreword
  1. Bahá'u'lláh, *Epistle to the Son of the Wolf*, p. 17.

Chapter 1. Overcoming Grief and Suffering
  1. 'Abdu'l-Bahá, in *Compilation*, vol. 2, p. 139.
  2. 'Abdu'l-Bahá, *Paris Talks*, p. 51.
  3. ibid. p. 178.
  4. ibid. p. 50.
  5. 'Abdu'l-Bahá, *Some Answered Questions*, p. 200.
  6. 'Abdu'l-Bahá, *Selections*, p. 239.
  7. 'Abdu'l-Bahá, *Paris Talks*, p. 178.

Chapter 2. Overcoming Anger and Hostility
  1. 'Abdu'l-Bahá, *Selections*, p. 3.
  2. Bahá'u'lláh, in *Compilation*, vol. 1, p. 460.
  3. 'Abdu'l-Bahá, *Selections*, p. 136.
  4. 'Abdu'l-Bahá, *Some Answered Questions*, p. 215.
  5. Bahá'u'lláh, *Tablets*, p. 36.
  6. ibid. p. 27.
  7. Bahá'u'lláh, *Gleanings*, p. 334.
  8. Bahá'u'lláh, *Hidden Words*, Arabic no. 27.
  9. 'Abdu'l-Bahá, *Promulgation*, p. 453.
 10. 'Abdu'l-Bahá, *Selections*, p. 3.
 11. ibid. p. 24.
 12. ibid. p. 34.
 13. ibid. p. 245.
 14. 'Abdu'l-Bahá, *Paris Talks*, p. 29.
 15. ibid. p. 30.

Chapter 3. Overcoming Fear

1. Bahá'u'lláh, *Epistle to the Son of the Wolf*, p. 32.
2. Bahá'u'lláh, *Tablets*, p. 190.
3. Bahá'u'lláh, 'The Four Valleys', in *Seven Valleys*, p. 58.
4. Bahá'u'lláh, *Gleanings*, p. 175.
5. 'Abdu'l-Bahá, *Selections*, pp. 17–18.
6. Bahá'u'lláh, 'Tablet of Aḥmad', in *Bahá'í Prayers*, p. 212.

Chapter 4. Developing Patience

1. Bahá'u'lláh, *Epistle to the Son of the Wolf*, p. 134.
2. Bahá'u'lláh, *Gleanings*, p. 129.
3. ibid. p. 120.
4. ibid. p. 290.
5. ibid. p. 296.
6. ibid. p. 239.
7. Bahá'u'lláh, *Epistle to the Son of the Wolf*, p. 24.
8. Bahá'u'lláh, *Tablets*, p. 138.
9. Bahá'u'lláh, *Seven Valleys*, p. 13.
10. The Báb, *Selections*, p. 161.
11. 'Abdu'l-Bahá, *Selections*, p. 74.
12. 'Abdu'l-Bahá, *Bahá'í World Faith*, p. 375.

Chapter 5. Developing Hope and Assurance

1. Bahá'u'lláh, *Gleanings*, p. 323.
2. ibid. p. 61.
3. 'Abdu'l-Bahá, *Selections*, p. 205.
4. Bahá'u'lláh, in Shoghi Effendi, *Advent of Divine Justice*, p. 82.
5. Words of the Báb to the Letters of the Living, in Nabíl-i-A'zam, *Dawn-Breakers*, p. 94.
6. Bahá'u'lláh, *Gleanings*, p. 106.
7. 'Abdu'l-Bahá, *Paris Talks*, p. 38.
8. ibid. p. 166.
9. 'Abdu'l-Bahá, *Selections*, p. 116.

Chapter 6. Using Prayer

1. Bahá'u'lláh, *Gleanings*, p. 265.
2. ibid. p. 295.
3. The Báb, *Selections*, p. 78.
4. 'Abdu'l-Bahá, *Promulgation*, p. 247.
5. 'Abdu'l-Bahá, *Paris Talks*, p. 57.
6. ibid. p. 61.
7. ibid. p. 111.
8. 'Abdu'l-Bahá, in *Bahá'í World Faith*, p. 368.
9. 'Abdu'l-Bahá, *Selections*, p. 202.
10. 'Abdu'l-Bahá, *Paris Talks*, p. 30.
11. 'Abdu'l-Bahá, in *Bahá'í World Faith*, p. 368.
12. 'Abdu'l-Bahá, *Selections*, p. 178.
13. Bahá'u'lláh, *Tablets*, p. 16.
14. The Báb, *Selections*, p. 217.
15. Bahá'u'lláh, *Prayers and Meditations*, pp. 262–3.
16. ibid. pp. 30–1.

Chapter 7. Healing

1. 'Abdu'l-Bahá, *Selections*, p. 151.
2. 'Abdu'l-Bahá, in *Bahá'í World Faith*, p. 376.
3. 'Abdu'l-Bahá, *Selections*, p. 152.
4. ibid. p. 23.
5. 'Abdu'l-Bahá, from a Tablet to Mme. L'Astre, in *Star of the West*, vol. 8, no. 18, p. 232.
6. 'Abdu'l-Bahá, *Paris Talks*, p. 19.
7. Bahá'u'lláh, *Gleanings*, p. 80.
8. ibid. p. 81.
9. ibid. pp. 156–7.

Chapter 8. The Next World

1. Bahá'u'lláh, *Gleanings*, pp. 155–7.
2. 'Abdu'l-Bahá, *Selections*, pp. 170–1.
3. ibid. p. 201.